T0197525

Christopher's New Suit

Written by Rose Brenda Lavis

Illustrated by Susan Anderson-Shorter

AuthorHouse™
1663 Liberty Drive
Bloomington, IN 47403
www.authorhouse.com
Phone: 833-262-8899

Because of the dynamic nature of the Internet, any web addresses or links contained in this book may have changed since publication and may no longer be valid. The views expressed in this work are solely those of the author and do not necessarily reflect the views of the publisher, and the publisher hereby disclaims any responsibility for them.

Any people depicted in stock imagery provided by Getty Images are models, and such images are being used for illustrative purposes only.
Certain stock imagery © Getty Images.

This book is printed on acid-free paper.

ISBN: 978-1-4490-3606-5 (sc)

Print information available on the last page.

Published by AuthorHouse 08/16/2023

authorHOUSE®

This book is dedicated to my children;
Christopher and Jill
and to my grandchildren;
Tyson, Kylan and Rayden.
You are the true wonders in my life.

Other Books by
Rose Brenda Lavis

The Girl Who Tamed Her Wonder Worm
Here Comes Trouble & Double Trouble
I'm Special
Rose's World (biography of the author; adult reading)

Christopher is seven-years-old and in the second grade. When Christopher was about four-and-a-half-years-old, before he started kindergarten, his dad asked him what he wanted to be when he grew up. Christopher thought about it and asked his dad, "what jobs make lots of money?"

His dad answered, "a doctor or a lawyer makes a lot of money." His dad added, "You know there are different types of lawyers." Christopher asked, "which kind of lawyer makes the most money?"

His dad answered, "a corporate lawyer." Christopher thought about it for a minute and said to his dad, "then I think I will be a corporate lawyer." His dad asked, "why a lawyer and not a doctor?" And Christopher answered, "Because they get to wear a suit!"

Christopher told his mother that he would like a suit. As this was an unusual request from a four-year-old his mother asked him, "and why would you like a suit?" Of course being four-and-a-half Christopher answered, "I don't know, I just want a suit."

Christopher's parents were not poor, but a suit was definitely an expense, which would have to be saved for. His mother did not know his reasons for wanting a suit. His father didn't have a suit. They did not go to church; it just did not seem practical to buy a suit for a four-year-old boy, who had no place to wear it. His mother assumed, as he was four, he would soon forget about wanting a suit.

Christopher never stopped wanting a suit. He asked for a suit when he started kindergarten. He was still asking for a suit in grade one. He never stopped asking for a suit.

One fall day Christopher came home after school. He was now in second grade. There; sitting in the living room were two large bags of new clothes.

Christopher had a neighbour who was three years older than he was. When Tommy out grew his clothes, Tommy's mother would pass them on to Christopher. Tommy's family was fairly well off and Tommy always had really nice clothes. Tommy's family went to church.

When Christopher opened the bags there it was! It wasn't a whole suit with a jacket but it was Tommy's tan dress pants and a matching vest.

Christopher was so excited! He had a suit! He didn't even look at the other clothes. His mother searched through the bags and found a shirt she thought would match.

Christopher just looked at her and said, "Mom, I can't wear that with my suit! It has to be a white shirt! Everybody knows you wear a white shirt with a suit." After searching through the remaining clothes there it was a white shirt!

Christopher said, "Great! All I need now is a tie." Christopher was so pleased with his suit and so sure that he could not wear it without a white shirt and tie his mother took him out to buy a tie.

The next morning Christopher was up early for school. He was already dressed in his suit and tie when his mother got up. He was so excited to be wearing his new suit to school.

His mother knew how important this was to Christopher and how excited he was. She also knew that children in second grade wear blue jeans and T-shirts to school and may not understand why Christopher was wearing a suit. A suit may be okay if it was picture day.

She thought she should prepare him for the other kid's reaction. She said, "you know Christopher; the other kids may notice that you are wearing a suit to school. They may say something. It is not every day they see a boy in a suit at school Christopher answered, "I know!" and hurried off to school.

Christopher returned home still wearing his suit. His mother thought perhaps he would come home upset with his tie in his pocket. She asked Christopher if the kids said anything about his suit. Christopher answered, "yeah-at first."

The children did laugh when they saw Christopher in his suit at school. Christopher didn't see anything funny about himself or his suit; but if they did it was okay if they laughed. Once the laughter was over the children continued to have a wonderful day at school.

Christopher did not know it but he used his POWER TOOL!

Christopher used his MIND, his POWER to CHOOSE his POWER to DECIDE.

He was an EMPOWERED person although he thought he was just an ordinary boy.

Christopher gave himself official power over himself.

He chose to value his own opinion over the other children's opinions.

He respected his own decision to wear his suit.

He also respected the other children's opinions and did not get upset or say anything nasty to the kids that laughed.

Christopher was EMPOWERED!!

Christopher would wear his suit to school whenever he chose to. Until one day he had grown too big for it to fit.

Christopher never out grew being EMPOWERED!

Christopher accepted that if the other children thought his suit was funny, it was okay if they laughed, and that children laughing did not change how special his suit was or how wonderful he felt every time he put it on. The children saw Christopher in his suit so often that no one even noticed anymore. It was only funny the first time because it was something different.

If you use your **POWER TOOL**, your **MIND**, every boy and girl can choose, can decide, and every boy and girl can be **EMPOWERED!!**. Whether something is a joy or a problem all depends on how you choose to look at it. Christopher chose to make his suit a joy and it was!

Christopher's new suit is a true story. Christopher is my son. Christopher grew to be an **EMPOWERED** man and is now teaching his son how to use his own **POWER TOOL BRAIN!!**

Christopher is not a lawyer but he does wear a suit. He now wears a whole suit jacket included.

THE END

Printed in the United States
by Baker & Taylor Publisher Services